The Science of Tao

CLAYTON TONKIN

DEDICATION

To my family—

For your love, support, and the lessons you've taught me, both spoken and unspoken.

For shaping me into the person I am today and reminding me of what truly matters.

For standing by me through every season of life, just as the Tao flows through all things.

This book is for you.

CONTENTS

ACKNOWLEDGMENTS

I would like to express my heartfelt gratitude to my family for their unwavering love and support throughout this journey. To my parents and siblings, who have always encouraged me to explore new ideas and perspectives, and to my cats, Dexter and Hamish, who have been a constant source of joy and inspiration. Your presence in my life is a reminder of the importance of balance, companionship, and living in harmony.

I also extend my deepest thanks to the teachings of Taoism. The wisdom passed down through centuries has been a guiding light, offering clarity in moments of uncertainty and teaching me how to live with less resistance and more flow. The Tao has not only shaped my thinking but has also transformed the way I experience the world. This book would not have been possible without the timeless wisdom of the Tao that continues to inspire and guide me. To the Tao, for showing me the way, and to those who have walked this path before me. May we continue to learn and grow in harmony with the flow of life.

1 A BRIDGE BETWEEN ANCIENT WISDOM AND MODERN SCIENCE

For thousands of years, Taoism has described a universe in constant motion, guided by unseen forces, flowing effortlessly in cycles of balance and change. It speaks of Qi—a vital energy that connects all things—of the interplay between Yin and Yang, and of the art of Wu Wei, or effortless action, through which one aligns with the natural rhythms of existence. But these concepts were not formulated in laboratories or based on scientific experiments; they arose from careful observation of nature, introspection, and philosophical inquiry.

Yet, in an era of quantum mechanics, energy fields, and vibrational science, we now find striking parallels between ancient Taoist teachings and modern physics. The very principles that Taoism describes—such as the interconnectedness of all things, the cyclical nature of existence, and the balance of opposing forces—are now supported by discoveries in quantum entanglement, thermodynamics, and cosmology. Scientists are uncovering what Taoist sages seemed to know intuitively: the universe is not a static, mechanical construct, but a dynamic, ever-changing flow of energy and information.

The Search for Patterns in The Universe

At its core, both Taoism and science seek to understand the patterns that govern existence. The Taoist view does not impose rigid laws or absolute truths but instead sees the world as an interconnected system, where everything influences everything else. This holistic approach resonates deeply with modern scientific fields like systems theory, chaos theory, and complexity science, which examine how order emerges from apparent randomness and how systems self-regulate.

Consider the Taoist principle of Wu Wei, often translated as "effortless action" or "going with the flow." While it may sound esoteric, modern physics has uncovered similar ideas in fluid dynamics and aerodynamics—where objects move most efficiently by reducing resistance rather than forcing their way through. The same applies to biological systems, from the way birds migrate using air currents to how our bodies optimize energy consumption.

Then there is Qi, the life force that Taoists believe pervades all existence. While Western science has long dismissed Qi as unprovable, recent research in bioelectricity, electromagnetic fields, and quantum field theory suggests that energy fields indeed influence life at every level. Whether in the form of electromagnetic radiation from the sun sustaining life on Earth or subatomic particles constantly interacting in a sea of quantum fluctuations, modern physics is beginning to describe a universe that behaves very much like the energetic, flowing cosmos Taoism envisions.

A Universe of Vibrations and Energy

One of the most fundamental discoveries of modern science is that everything vibrates. Atoms, molecules, sound waves, light waves, and even the neural activity in our brains—all are oscillating patterns of energy. Taoism, too, sees the universe as a field of flowing energy, where balance and resonance play a key role in health, harmony, and transformation.

Scientific breakthroughs in wave-particle duality, frequency resonance, and quantum coherence are revealing that the material world is not as solid as it seems. At the smallest scales, particles behave more like waves of probability, constantly fluctuating and interacting. These discoveries align with the Taoist idea that reality is fluid, ever-changing, and shaped by unseen forces.

Is Taoism A Science?

At first glance, Taoism and science might seem like opposing worldviews. Science relies on empirical data, mathematical models, and experimental verification, while Taoism emphasizes intuition, natural observation, and philosophical reflection. However, they share a fundamental similarity: both seek to uncover the deeper principles that govern reality.

While Taoism does not follow the scientific method, it offers a framework for understanding patterns in nature, much like science does. It recognizes that nature operates through self-organizing principles, much like how scientists describe emergence in complex systems. The Taoist view of balance and change mirrors the way scientists describe equilibrium in ecosystems, entropy in thermodynamics, and the feedback loops that regulate the cosmos.

The key difference is that while science often seeks to control or manipulate nature, Taoism teaches us to align with it. Rather than resisting the natural flow of life, Taoist philosophy encourages harmony and adaptation, principles that are now being recognized as essential for sustainable living, ecological balance, and even psychological well-being.

Bridging The Gap Between East and West

For centuries, Western thought has been dominated by a mechanistic view of the universe—one that sees nature as a system of discrete, separate parts that operate according to fixed laws. However, modern physics is shifting towards a more holistic understanding, one that sees interconnection, uncertainty, and fluidity as fundamental aspects of reality.

Quantum mechanics has revealed that particles can be entangled across vast distances, meaning they are instantaneously connected no matter how far apart they are—a notion that strongly echoes the Taoist belief in universal oneness. Similarly, the observer effect, which suggests that consciousness plays a role in shaping reality, raises profound questions about the nature of existence—questions that Taoist philosophy has been pondering for millennia.

This book is not about mysticism or pseudoscience, nor is it an attempt to force scientific discoveries to fit ancient spiritual ideas. Rather, it is an exploration of how Taoist wisdom and modern science seem to be converging, offering a deeper understanding of the world we live in.

What You'll Discover in This Book

Each chapter of this book will dive into a different aspect of how Taoist concepts align with scientific discoveries:

- **Chapter 1** will introduce the core principles of Taoism—Tao, Qi, Yin-Yang, and Wu Wei—and how they describe the natural flow of the universe.

- **Chapter 2** will examine the concept of Qi and its possible scientific parallels in energy fields and bioelectricity.

- **Chapter 3** will explore the science of vibrations, frequencies, and resonance, showing how everything moves and interacts through waves.

- **Chapter 4** will delve into the duality of Yin-Yang and its reflections in physics, from wave-particle duality to chaos and order.

- **Chapter 5** will reveal how Wu Wei aligns with principles of efficiency, flow states, and the physics of minimal resistance.

- **Chapter 6** will examine the links between Taoism and quantum mechanics, exploring uncertainty, the observer effect, and nonlocality.

- **Chapter 7** will discuss the interconnectedness of all things, drawing on quantum entanglement and systems theory.

- **Chapter 8** will offer insights into Taoist health practices and their scientific basis, from breathwork to bioelectric energy.

- **Chapter 9** will connect Taoist cosmology with astrophysical cycles, the expansion and contraction of the universe, and the nature of time.

- **Chapter 10** will tie everything together, offering practical applications for how we can live in harmony with the flow of nature.

The Science of Tao: A New Perspective on Reality

We are at an exciting crossroads where ancient wisdom and cutting-edge science are beginning to speak the same language. The Tao, once seen as a purely mystical idea, may turn out to be a profound insight into the underlying forces that shape reality.

Through this book, we will explore whether the Tao can be scientifically understood—not as a supernatural force, but as a principle that governs the flow of energy, the balance of forces, and the evolution of the cosmos.

Are we discovering Taoism through science, or has Taoism been describing the universe all along?

Let's begin the journey.

2 WHAT IS TAO? THE FLOW OF ALL THINGS

Defining Tao: Beyond Religion, Beyond Word

The word Tao (道) is often translated as "The Way," but this definition barely scratches the surface. Tao is not just a spiritual concept, a deity, or a set of religious rules—it is a fundamental principle of existence, a force that governs the natural flow of all things. It is the movement of the cosmos, the rising and falling of tides, the rhythm of the seasons, and even the way a river carves its path through a mountain over time.

Laozi, the legendary sage and author of the Tao Te Ching, opens his text with a paradox:

> *"The Tao that can be spoken is not the eternal Tao."*

This suggests that Tao is beyond language and intellectual grasp. It is not something that can be fully defined or contained in words—it must be experienced. Yet, despite this ineffability, Taoists throughout history have attempted to describe it through metaphors and natural imagery, pointing to its ever-present influence in the world.

From a modern scientific perspective, this idea resonates

with certain fundamental principles of physics. Much like the laws of nature, the Tao is not a tangible thing that one can see or measure directly, yet it governs the motion of galaxies, the behaviour of subatomic particles, and the patterns of life itself.

The Origin of Taoism: Its Emphasis on Harmony

Taoism emerged in ancient China as a philosophy deeply rooted in observing nature. Unlike many Western philosophical traditions that focus on logic and reason, Taoism developed from studying how the world moves and adapts effortlessly. The early Taoists looked at the way trees bend in the wind without breaking, how rivers flow around obstacles instead of fighting against them, and how animals survive by blending with their environment.

From these observations, Taoists concluded that life is most harmonious when it follows the natural order rather than resisting it. This perspective gave birth to several key Taoist principles:

Wu Wei (Effortless Action): The idea that the best way to act is by aligning with the natural flow of circumstances rather than forcing things. This does not mean inaction, but rather a state of action without resistance.

Yin-Yang (Duality and Balance): The principle that opposites are interconnected and dependent on each other— light and dark, order and chaos, motion and stillness.

Qi (Life Energy): The concept that all living things and even inanimate objects possess a form of energy that flows through them, connecting everything in the universe.

Taoism and the Fundamental Principle

Science, like Taoism, has always sought to understand the fundamental nature of reality. While Taoism describes the universe as an interwoven flow, modern physics has also moved away from the idea of a rigid, mechanical world toward a more dynamic and relational understanding.

For example, classical Newtonian physics once saw the universe as a collection of discrete objects moving according to fixed laws. However, discoveries in quantum mechanics and relativity reveal a reality that is far more interconnected and fluid. The Higgs field, for instance, is an invisible energy field that pervades the universe, giving mass to particles—a concept reminiscent of the Tao as an omnipresent force. Similarly, the second law of thermodynamics, which describes how energy flows from order to disorder, mirrors the Taoist idea that all things are in constant change.

In a way, both Taoism and modern physics suggest that the universe operates not through rigid control, but through patterns of movement and balance. The Tao is not a lawgiver like a deity, nor is it a force that compels things in a fixed direction. Instead, it is the underlying flow that shapes everything naturally—just as gravity shapes rivers, or as the curvature of space-time guides planets in their orbits.

Taoism's Core Ideas and Their Scientific Parallels

Wu Wei and the Principle of Least Action

One of the most important ideas in Taoism is Wu Wei, often translated as "effortless action." It suggests that the most effective way to navigate life is to move with the natural currents of the universe rather than against them. Science has an equivalent concept: the principle of least action in physics.

This principle states that in nature, objects and energy always follow the path of least resistance. Light, for example, takes the shortest possible route between two points (Fermat's principle). Similarly, rivers carve paths that minimize energy expenditure, and planets orbit in ways that optimize their energy efficiency.

This is exactly what Wu Wei describes—not passivity, but a state of natural efficiency where things flow with minimal wasted effort.

Yin-Yang and Wave-Particle Duality

The Taoist symbol of Yin-Yang represents the balance of

opposites: light and dark, order and chaos, movement and stillness. This is not just philosophy—it reflects a fundamental truth of physics.

In quantum mechanics, the wave-particle duality of light and matter demonstrates that things can exist in seemingly opposite states at once. Light behaves both as a wave and as a particle, depending on how we observe it—just as Yin and Yang are not separate forces but two aspects of the same whole.

Furthermore, the principle of superposition in quantum physics suggests that particles exist in multiple states simultaneously until they interact with an observer. This fluidity between states is strikingly similar to the Taoist idea that reality is not fixed, but ever-changing and shaped by perspective.

Qi and the Science of Energy Fields

The Taoist concept of Qi (氣) is often misunderstood as a mystical or supernatural force. However, in a scientific context, Qi can be compared to various forms of energy fields that permeate the universe.

Modern science recognizes that energy is the foundation of all physical reality. The electromagnetic field, for example, exists everywhere, influencing the movement of charged particles. The zero-point energy field in quantum physics suggests that even empty space is filled with fluctuating energy. Some researchers speculate that biological systems are also influenced by subtle energy interactions, which may explain phenomena such as bioelectricity, neural conductivity, and the body's response to electromagnetic frequencies.

While Qi may not yet have a direct scientific explanation, the idea that energy flows through and connects all things is a core principle of both Taoism and modern physics.

The Flow of All Things: Tao in Everyday Life

If Tao is the natural flow of the universe, what does this mean for us on a practical level? It means that fighting against reality—whether in nature, relationships, or personal struggles—often leads to frustration and exhaustion. When we accept and adapt instead of resisting, we align ourselves with the natural rhythm of life. This is why Taoism emphasizes fluidity, adaptability, and acceptance of change.

A surfer does not fight the ocean but rides the waves, adjusting to their rhythm.

A tree does not resist the wind but bends with it, preventing itself from breaking.

A scientist does not impose their will on nature but seeks to understand its patterns.

These are all manifestations of the Tao at work. By learning to recognize the flow of nature, we can find greater ease, clarity, and harmony in our own lives.

Tao As a Universal Principle

Taoism is not a religion in the conventional sense—it is a way of seeing and interacting with the world. In many ways, it aligns with modern science's search for an underlying order in the cosmos.

Whether we look at physics, biology, or human behaviour, we find the same patterns: flow, balance, adaptation, and interconnectedness. The Tao may not be a force we can measure in a laboratory, but its effects are seen everywhere—from the tiniest subatomic interactions to the vast structure of galaxies.

Understanding Tao is not about believing in something mystical, but about observing reality as it is—and learning to move with it, rather than against it.

In the next chapter, we will explore the concept of Qi, and whether science has begun to uncover its hidden energies.

3 HIDDEN ENERGIES OF THE UNIVERSE

Qi: The Lifeblood of Taoism

In Taoist philosophy, Qi (氣) is the fundamental energy that flows through all things. It is the breath of life, the unseen force that animates existence, and the connective thread between the physical and the immaterial. Unlike Western concepts of energy, which are often defined in strictly mechanical or measurable terms, Qi is understood as a living, dynamic force—one that moves through the body, the earth, and the cosmos itself.

Ancient Chinese texts describe Qi in various forms:

- **Tian Qi (天氣):** The energy of the heavens, influencing weather, cosmic movements, and celestial balance.

- **Di Qi (地氣):** The energy of the earth, affecting fertility, natural cycles, and the landscape.

- **Ren Qi (人氣):** The energy within human beings, governing health, vitality, and consciousness.

For centuries, sceptics dismissed Qi as a mystical or metaphysical concept with no basis in science. However, modern discoveries in physics, biology, and neuroscience suggest that Qi may not be as unscientific as once thought. The study of energy fields, bioelectricity, and quantum interactions reveals that invisible forces do indeed shape reality—and, in many ways, they align with the Taoist understanding of Qi.

Does Science Support the Concept of Qi?

To bridge the gap between Taoist tradition and scientific inquiry, we must ask: What is Qi in scientific terms? While there is no single answer, several fields of study provide compelling parallels.

Qi and the Electromagnetic Field

One of the closest scientific equivalents to Qi is the electromagnetic field (EMF)—a force that permeates all of space, influencing everything from atoms to galaxies. The human body itself generates its own electromagnetic fields, most notably in the heart and brain.

The heart produces the strongest electromagnetic field in the body, extending several feet beyond the skin. Neurons communicate through bioelectrical signals, transmitting thoughts and emotions. Even at a cellular level, tiny electrical currents govern essential biological functions.

Taoist practices such as Qi Gong, Tai Chi, and acupuncture are believed to influence Qi flow, but modern science suggests they may actually be interacting with the body's bioelectrical system. For example, research has shown that acupuncture points correspond to areas of lower electrical resistance in the skin, suggesting a link between ancient energy pathways and modern neurophysiology.

The Zero-Point Energy Field: Qi on a Cosmic Scale

Another scientific concept that bears resemblance to Qi is zero-point energy—the idea that even in the vacuum of empty space, energy fluctuations are constantly occurring. In quantum physics, this means that the universe is never truly "empty"; it is filled with a field of underlying energy that exists

12

even at absolute zero temperature.

This aligns with the Taoist belief that Qi is omnipresent and ever-moving, even when it appears still. It suggests that there is no true "nothingness"—only unseen energy waiting to manifest. Some physicists speculate that zero-point energy may even be responsible for dark energy, the mysterious force driving the expansion of the universe.

Bioelectricity: The Body's Internal Qi Flow
Traditional Chinese medicine teaches that Qi flows through meridians—pathways that guide energy throughout the body. While meridians have long been considered an unproven idea, new research suggests they may correspond to fascia networks and bioelectrical pathways in the body.

Fascia is a thin layer of connective tissue that surrounds muscles, organs, and nerves. It is now understood to play a key role in electrical conductivity within the body. Some studies suggest that water molecules within the fascia can store and transmit electrical charges, creating a network of energy transfer much like the meridians described in Chinese medicine.

Additionally, the piezoelectric effect, a phenomenon where mechanical pressure generates electrical energy, may explain how movement-based practices like Tai Chi stimulate bioelectric flow. Every time we stretch, contract, or twist our bodies, electrical signals are generated—just as Taoist practitioners have long claimed Qi is activated through movement.

Ancient Energy Practices: Aligning with Qi

If Qi is indeed connected to bioelectricity and energy fields, then it is no surprise that Taoist practices developed ways to cultivate and control it. These methods, once seen as purely mystical, now have scientific backing.

Qi Gong and Bioelectromagnetic Regulation
Qi Gong is a set of movement, breathing, and meditation techniques designed to enhance Qi flow. Studies on Qi Gong

practitioners show measurable changes in heart rate variability, brainwave activity, and electromagnetic field output—all indicators that Qi Gong may regulate the body's electrical and physiological balance.

One particularly striking study from the National Institutes of Health (NIH) found that Qi Gong practitioners could significantly alter their alpha and theta brainwave states, inducing a state of deep relaxation and heightened awareness. This suggests that Qi Gong may help synchronize the nervous system with natural energy rhythms, promoting overall well-being.

Acupuncture: Unlocking the Body's Electrical Pathways

Acupuncture, a practice based on inserting thin needles into Qi meridians, has been a cornerstone of Chinese medicine for thousands of years. While Western medicine once dismissed it as placebo, modern research shows that acupuncture points align with areas of high electrical conductivity and dense nerve endings.

MRI scans of acupuncture treatments reveal that stimulation of certain points can activate specific brain regions, influencing pain perception, mood, and even immune function. Some scientists believe that acupuncture modulates the body's bioelectric field, restoring balance in the same way that Qi is said to flow through meridians.

Breathwork and Oxygen-Energy Conversion

Breath is considered the most immediate and accessible form of Qi regulation. Taoists have long practiced deep, conscious breathing to cultivate vitality, and modern science confirms that breathing patterns directly impact oxygen levels, CO_2 balance, and energy metabolism.

Slow, controlled breathing enhances parasympathetic nervous system activity, reducing stress and increasing cellular oxygenation. Additionally, recent research on the Bohr effect (the relationship between CO_2 and oxygen absorption in the blood) suggests that breathwork practices optimize energy efficiency in the body—mirroring Taoist teachings on Qi flow through breath.

Qi As the Bridge Between Matter and Energy

The study of Qi, bioelectromagnetism, and quantum energy fields suggests that reality is not just made of solid matter, but of interwoven energy flows. This echoes the discoveries of quantum mechanics, which reveal that particles exist not as static objects, but as vibrating energy fields that constantly interact with their environment.

In essence, Qi is not a contradiction to science—it is a poetic description of the energetic nature of reality. The ancient Taoists may not have had electron microscopes or particle accelerators, but they intuited that the universe operates through invisible flows of energy rather than fixed structures.

The Hidden Science of Qi

For centuries, Western science and Eastern philosophy have taken different approaches to understanding energy. While Taoists spoke of Qi as an ever-moving life force, scientists measured energy through fields, waves, and particles. However, as modern research continues to unveil bioelectricity, electromagnetic fields, and quantum energy, the gap between Taoist wisdom and scientific understanding is beginning to close.

Qi may not be a force that can be weighed or bottled, but its effects can be observed, cultivated, and even measured in the body and the universe. Whether we look at acupuncture, breathwork, or bioelectric flow, we see that Qi is not just a mystical belief—it is a living, dynamic energy that shapes all things.

In the next chapter, we will explore how vibrations, frequencies, and resonance play a role in shaping reality—revealing how everything, from atoms to galaxies, moves in harmony with the Tao.

4 THE SCIENCE OF VIBRATIONS— EVERYTHING MOVES

The Universe Is in Motion

From the smallest subatomic particles to the largest cosmic structures, everything in the universe is in a state of constant movement. What appears to be still is simply moving at a frequency beyond our perception. This idea, deeply embedded in Taoist philosophy, aligns perfectly with modern science, which reveals that the fundamental nature of reality is vibration.

Taoists have long understood the universe as an interconnected web of flowing energy. The Tao Te Ching states,

> *"The Tao is empty yet inexhaustible,*
> *the more it is used, the more it*
> *produces."*

This reflects the idea that existence is not static but a continuous process of movement and transformation. Today, physics, biology, and even neuroscience confirm this principle: everything we perceive as solid, stable, or fixed is actually composed of vibrating energy fields.

Atoms vibrate. The electrons within an atom never stop moving, constantly shifting and oscillating around the nucleus.

Molecules vibrate. The bonds between atoms stretch and contract at specific frequencies, defining their behaviour.

Cells vibrate. The proteins in our body are in constant motion, influencing biological function at the microscopic level.

Planets vibrate. The Earth itself resonates with a natural frequency, known as the Schumann resonance.

Understanding how these vibrations shape reality allows us to bridge the wisdom of Taoist thought with the discoveries of modern science.

Resonance and Frequency: The Tao of Energy

Taoism teaches that balance and harmony arise when things are in sync with their natural flow. In physics, this concept is closely related to resonance—the principle that everything has a natural frequency at which it vibrates most efficiently.

What Is Frequency?

In scientific terms, frequency refers to the number of times something vibrates per second, measured in Hertz (Hz).

A low-frequency wave moves slowly, like deep ocean waves or the rolling sound of a drum.

A high-frequency wave moves rapidly, like the sharp note of a violin string or gamma rays in space.

Each object, from a grain of sand to a galaxy, has a natural vibrational frequency. When an external force matches this frequency, resonance occurs, amplifying the object's movement. A classic example is a singer shattering a glass by hitting the precise pitch that resonates with the glass's structure.

Vibrations and the Flow of the Tao
In Taoism, harmony is achieved when we align with the natural flow of energy rather than resisting it. Science confirms this in many ways:

Heart and Brain Coherence: Studies show that when our heart rate and brainwaves sync up, we experience states of flow, creativity, and relaxation—a modern reflection of Taoist Wu Wei (effortless action).

Music and Healing: Certain sound frequencies, such as 432 Hz or 528 Hz, are believed to have calming and healing effects, aligning with the idea that sound vibrations can restore balance in the body.

Ecosystems and Nature's Rhythms: The vibrations of living organisms influence entire ecosystems, from the way bees communicate through vibrations to how plants respond to sound frequencies.

Taoism has always emphasized adapting to the natural rhythms of the universe. When we fight against the flow, we create resistance. When we move with it, we experience harmony.

Wave-Particle Duality: Yin-Yang in Physics
One of the most profound discoveries in modern physics is wave-particle duality, which states that particles can behave as both solid objects and energy waves. This principle, first revealed through the double-slit experiment, mirrors the Yin-Yang philosophy of Taoism:

Yang (Particle): The tangible, measurable aspect of matter—structured, defined, and observable.

Yin (Wave): The intangible, flowing aspect—formless,

changing, and interconnected.

This paradox is at the heart of quantum mechanics, showing that reality is not fixed but depends on how we interact with it—an idea that resonates deeply with Taoist teachings.

The Role of Vibrations in Human Consciousness

Taoist meditation, Qi Gong, and breathwork are designed to attune the body to a state of balanced vibration. Modern research into brainwave states suggests that these practices may influence the brain's natural frequencies, shifting our consciousness in measurable ways.

Beta waves (13-30 Hz): Active thinking, problem-solving, and stress states.

Alpha waves (8-12 Hz): Relaxation, meditation, and creative flow.

Theta waves (4-7 Hz): Deep meditation, intuition, and subconscious awareness.

Delta waves (0.5-3 Hz): Deep sleep and cellular regeneration.

Practices such as mantras, chanting, and breath synchronization are believed to alter these brainwave states, helping individuals access deeper levels of consciousness. The

Science of Sound: Vibrations Influence Matter

One of the most fascinating ways that vibrations shape reality is through cymatics—the study of how sound frequencies create patterns in physical materials. When sound waves pass through substances like water or sand, they form intricate, geometric shapes, revealing that sound has the power to organize matter.

In Taoist philosophy, this is reflected in the belief that the universe is created through vibration and movement, not static form. In modern science, it supports the idea that energy frequencies shape the material world. Experiments with cymatics suggest that our environment, our thoughts, and even our emotions—each associated with specific frequencies—may have the ability to shape the physical reality around us.

Tuning Ourselves to the Frequency of Nature

Taoism teaches that the key to well-being is aligning with natural rhythms. Whether in music, breath, movement, or thought, vibrations influence every aspect of our existence.

Breathing in rhythm with nature's cycles can enhance energy and clarity. Listening to harmonious sounds and frequencies can calm the nervous system. Moving in fluid, natural ways (Tai Chi, dance, or even simple stretching) helps restore balance in the body. In the same way that a well-tuned instrument plays beautiful music, a well-tuned life flows effortlessly with the Tao.

Vibrations as the Foundation of Reality

Modern physics, neuroscience, and biology confirm what Taoism has long taught: existence is a dance of energy, waves, and frequencies. Every thought, every action, and every aspect of nature resonates at a specific vibration, shaping reality moment by moment.

Understanding these principles allows us to move with the natural currents of the universe, rather than struggling against them. Whether through sound, breath, movement, or consciousness, we can cultivate a life in harmony with the vibrational nature of reality—living in effortless flow with the Tao.

In the next chapter, we will explore Yin-Yang and the fundamental duality of the universe, examining how the balance of opposites shapes everything from physics and biology to human relationships and cosmic cycles.

5 YIN-YANG AND THE DUALITY OF THE UNIVERSE

The Cosmic Dance of Opposites

At the heart of Taoist philosophy lies the concept of Yin and Yang, the interplay of opposites that gives rise to all existence. Light and dark, motion and stillness, creation and destruction—these forces are not in conflict but in harmony, constantly shifting in a dynamic balance. The Tao Te Ching describes it poetically:

> *"Under heaven, all can see beauty as beauty only because there is ugliness. All can know good as good only because there is evil. Being and non-being create each other. Difficult and easy support each other. Long and short define each other. High and low depend on each other."*

Modern science mirrors this ancient wisdom. Physics, biology, and even cosmology are built on duality—opposing yet complementary forces that shape the natural world. Whether in the push-pull of electromagnetism, the cycle of life and death, or the dual nature of subatomic particles, the balance of Yin and Yang is evident everywhere.

Yin-Yang in Science: The Balance of Forces

While Taoists expressed Yin and Yang poetically, science provides a measurable framework for these dualities. Below are some of the key scientific parallels to this fundamental Taoist principle.

Electromagnetism

The Attraction of Opposites One of the most basic forces in physics, electromagnetism, operates on the principle of Yin-Yang balance. Positive and negative charges exist in everything from atoms to planetary fields. Magnetic poles attract and repel, forming the invisible energy networks that guide compasses and control the Sun's activity. Light itself is a Yin-Yang force, composed of electric (Yang) and magnetic (Yin) waves that oscillate together to create electromagnetic radiation.

Without this duality, the universe would collapse. The balance between attraction and repulsion is what holds matter together while also allowing energy to flow freely—echoing the Taoist idea that opposing forces are both necessary and interdependent.

Matter and Antimatter

The Cosmic Yin-Yang In modern physics, the idea of opposites extends beyond electromagnetism. The matter-antimatter duality is one of the great mysteries of the universe. For every particle, there exists an antiparticle—an opposite version with the same mass but opposite charge. When matter and antimatter meet, they annihilate, releasing pure energy in the form of light.

The Big Bang is believed to have produced equal amounts of matter and antimatter, yet for some unknown reason, matter slightly outweighed antimatter—allowing the universe as we know it to exist.

Taoism teaches that in every extreme lies the seed of its opposite. If perfect symmetry had existed, matter and antimatter would have cancelled each other out, and the cosmos would be nothing but empty radiation. Instead, a tiny imbalance—a sliver of Yang in the sea of Yin—allowed everything to unfold.

The Chaos-Order Cycle: The Universe's Natural Rhythm
The second law of thermodynamics states that entropy (disorder) always increases over time. However, within this process, pockets of order emerge—like planets forming from cosmic dust or life evolving from chaos.

Yang (Order): Stars, galaxies, and life itself arise from structured complexity.

Yin (Chaos): Over time, disorder grows—stars burn out, galaxies collide, and all things decay.

This mirrors the Taoist belief that Yin and Yang are never static—they constantly flow into each other. A rigid system collapses, while an overly chaotic system never produces anything stable. The secret of longevity, both in nature and in human life, is learning how to move with the rhythm of change rather than resisting it

Yin-Yang in Biology: Life's Dual Nature
Nature's cycles follow the same pattern of opposites in balance. From cellular processes to ecosystems, life thrives by maintaining a dynamic equilibrium.

The Sympathetic and Parasympathetic Nervous Systems
In our bodies, the nervous system operates on a Yin- Yang principle:

Sympathetic (Yang): The fight-or-flight system, activated during stress, increases heart rate and energy production.

Parasympathetic (Yin): The rest-and-digest system, which slows the heart rate and promotes relaxation.

A balance between the two is crucial for health. Too much Yang (stress, overwork) leads to burnout, while too much Yin (stagnation, lethargy) leads to weakness. Taoist practices like Qi Gong, Tai Chi, and meditation help regulate this balance, mirroring modern neuroscience's understanding of stress management and recovery cycles.

DNA and the Dual Helix of Life

The very structure of DNA, the blueprint of life, reflects Yin-Yang balance. DNA exists as a double helix—two strands twisting around each other in perfect harmony. One strand serves as a template (Yin), while the other encodes genetic instructions (Yang). Without this dual structure, life as we know it wouldn't function.

Much like Taoist philosophy, biology teaches that opposites do not compete—they complement each other to create something greater than the sum of their parts.

The Yin-Yang of Human Emotions and Behaviour

Beyond the physical world, the concept of Yin and Yang applies to human psychology, relationships, and decision-making.

Logic vs. Intuition: The left brain (Yang) is analytical, while the right brain (Yin) is creative and intuitive. True intelligence integrates both.

Action vs. Rest: Society often glorifies constant action (Yang), but true productivity requires periods of rest (Yin) to recharge.

Independence vs. Connection: A life focused only on independence (Yang) can lead to isolation, while too much dependence (Yin) can lead to stagnation. Healthy relationships balance both.

This is why Taoist wisdom emphasizes flow over force. Trying to suppress emotions, ignore natural rhythms, or control every outcome creates imbalance. Instead, recognizing and accepting the dual nature of existence leads to inner peace and adaptability.

Expansion and Contraction of the Universe

Even on a cosmic scale, Yin and Yang are at play in the grandest cycle of all—the fate of the universe itself.

Yang (Expansion): Since the Big Bang, the universe has been expanding outward at an accelerating rate.

Yin (Contraction): Some theories suggest that eventually, this expansion may slow and reverse, leading to a Big Crunch—a collapse back into a singularity, only for the cycle to begin again.

Taoism teaches that the universe is cyclical, not linear. Whether through the orbit of planets, the rise and fall of civilizations, or the inhale and exhale of a breath, everything follows the rhythm of expansion and contraction—creation and dissolution.

Finding Balance in a Dualistic World

Yin and Yang are not just abstract symbols—they are laws of nature. From the forces that shape the cosmos to the chemistry of our own bodies, this interplay of opposites governs everything.

Understanding this can transform how we live:
- Instead of resisting change, we learn to flow with it.
- Instead of chasing extremes, we find equilibrium.
- Instead of seeing opposites as enemies, we recognize them as partners in the dance of existence.

In the next chapter, we will explore Wu Wei—the art of effortless action, and how the laws of physics and neuroscience support the Taoist idea that true power comes not from force, but from flow.

6 WU WEI AND THE PHYSICS OF FLOW

The Power of Effortless Action

Imagine a leaf floating down a river. It does not struggle against the current or force its direction—it simply moves with the water, adjusting effortlessly to twists, turns, and obstacles.

This is Wu Wei (无为), one of the core principles of Taoism, often translated as "effortless action" or "non-forcing."

At first glance, Wu Wei may seem like passivity or laziness, but in reality, it is the opposite. It is not inaction, but aligned action—a state where effort and movement occur in perfect harmony with the natural flow of life. Laozi describes it in the Tao Te Ching:

> *"The soft overcomes the hard.*
>
> *The gentle overcomes the rigid.*
>
> *The Tao never strives, yet nothing is*
> *left undone."*

In modern science, this idea of working with natural forces rather than against them is not just philosophy—it is a fundamental principle in physics, biology, psychology, and even human performance. Whether it's water flowing effortlessly around rocks, athletes entering a state of peak performance, or organizations adapting seamlessly to change, Wu Wei finds its scientific validation in the concept of flow, efficiency, and minimal resistance.

The Physics of Wu Wei: Path of Lease Resistance

In physics, the idea of minimizing resistance and maximizing efficiency is essential to understanding how nature operates. Many of the fundamental forces of the universe naturally align with the principle of Wu Wei.

Hydrodynamics: The Taoist metaphor of water perfectly illustrates Wu Wei. Water does not fight obstacles; it flows around them, over time shaping entire landscapes. This principle is mirrored in fluid dynamics, where systems always seek the most efficient, least resistant path.

Laminar Flow vs. Turbulent Flow: In laminar flow, water moves smoothly and efficiently. In turbulent flow, resistance increases, causing disorder and wasted energy. Wu Wei aligns with laminar flow—adapting to conditions rather than resisting them.

Erosion and Adaptation: Rivers carve mountains not through force, but through persistence and flexibility. Over time, even the hardest rock is shaped by the gentle but relentless movement of water—a direct analogy to the power of effortless persistence.

Thermodynamics: The Universe Seeks Equilibrium The second law of thermodynamics states that systems naturally move toward equilibrium—a state where energy is distributed evenly, without excessive force or waste. Heat moves from hot to cold until balance is achieved. Air flows from high pressure to low pressure without force. This reflects Wu Wei on a cosmic scale.

The universe expands according to gravitational

equilibrium, seeking the most efficient structure. Wu Wei teaches that we, too, should align ourselves with natural balance rather than fight against it. Resistance creates struggle, while harmony creates ease.

Wu Wei and the Science of Human Flow States

The idea of effortless action is not just found in physics—it is also the key to peak human performance. Modern neuroscience describes a similar state called flow, in which people perform at their best with minimal conscious effort.

The Neuroscience of Flow

Psychologist Mihály Csíkszentmihályi defined flow as the state where a person is completely absorbed in an activity, experiencing effortless concentration and peak performance. This is the scientific equivalent of Wu Wei. When in flow, brain activity shifts, reducing activity in the prefrontal cortex (the part responsible for overthinking and self-doubt). The brain releases dopamine, endorphins, and norepinephrine, increasing motivation and focus. Athletes, artists, and musicians describe this state as "being in the zone", where everything feels effortless yet precise. Just as a river does not need to "try" to flow, a person in a flow state acts without excessive effort—just pure, aligned action.

Wu Wei in Sports and Martial Arts

Athletes often describe moments of peak performance as effortless movement, where they react without thinking. This is a direct parallel to Wu Wei.

In martial arts, rigidity leads to defeat. Fighters who are too tense or overthink their movements get exhausted. The best fighters move fluidly, adapting to their opponent's energy. In basketball or soccer, elite players don't force movements— they flow naturally, reading the game intuitively. In free diving, world-record divers describe how fighting water leads to panic, but surrendering to the ocean leads to deeper, more successful dives.

Wu Wei is the ability to let go of control, trust in natural movement, and achieve effortless mastery.

Wu Wei in Psychology: Adaptability and Resilience

Beyond sports, Wu Wei is also seen in mental well-being and adaptability.

The Paradox of Control: The more you force, the more you struggle. Wu Wei suggests that forcing control over situations often backfires. Modern psychology supports this.

The Paradox of Anxiety: Trying to control every outcome leads to stress. Letting go and trusting the process reduces anxiety.

Creative Flow: Writers, musicians, and artists produce their best work when they stop trying too hard and let inspiration guide them.

Decision-Making: Studies show that overthinking often leads to worse decisions. Wu Wei suggests trusting intuition and natural timing.

The key is alignment over force—like a surfer riding a wave instead of fighting against it.

Wu Wei in Leadership and Social Dynamics

Great leaders and effective teams also embody Wu Wei. Forcing control often creates resistance, while influencing through alignment creates natural movement.

Micromanaging (forcing control) leads to stress and inefficiency. Trusting employees (Wu Wei) leads to better productivity and innovation. Negotiations work best when both sides feel heard, rather than one forcing an outcome. The best leaders, artists, and innovators understand this truth: The secret to great action is effortless action.

Wu Wei and the Tao of Everyday Life

Wu Wei is not just for physics, neuroscience, or sports—it applies to how we live, love, and make decisions.

In work: Instead of forcing productivity, create the right conditions for natural focus and creativity.

In relationships: Forcing control in relationships leads to resistance. Letting things flow naturally builds deeper connections.

In health: Forcing extreme diets or exercise regimens often fails. But moving naturally, eating intuitively, and listening to the body lead to lasting health.

In problem-solving: Instead of forcing solutions, step back, observe, and allow insights to emerge naturally.

Taoist masters, athletes, scientists, and artists all arrive at the same truth—when you align with the natural flow, things happen effortlessly.

The Science of Going with the Flow

Wu Wei is not magic—it is a principle backed by science and nature. The universe, from fluid dynamics to human performance, shows us that effortless action is not the absence of effort—it is the presence of perfect alignment.

Water flows around obstacles—it does not resist. The brain performs best when in flow, not when forcing. Athletes, artists, and leaders succeed not by controlling, but by adapting.

In the next chapter, we will explore how this idea of effortless alignment extends to quantum physics, where the act of observation itself influences reality—further proving that true power is not in force, but in flow.

7 QUANTUM TAO—THE OBSERVER AND THE UNCERTAINTY PRINCIPLE

Does the Universe Respond to Awareness?
For centuries, Taoism has emphasized the idea that reality is fluid, shaped by balance, interconnectedness, and perception. The Tao Te Ching states:

> *"The Tao that can be spoken is not the eternal Tao. The name that can be named is not the eternal name."*

This suggests that reality itself is elusive, shifting based on how we interact with it. Strangely enough, modern quantum physics echoes this exact sentiment. Scientists have discovered that at the smallest levels of existence—within the realm of subatomic particles—reality does not behave in a fixed or predictable way. Instead, it changes based on how we observe it. This idea is best demonstrated by two key discoveries in quantum mechanics:

The Observer Effect: The act of measuring a quantum system alters its behaviour.

The Heisenberg Uncertainty Principle: It is impossible

to precisely determine both the position and momentum of a particle at the same time.

These discoveries suggest that conscious observation might play a role in shaping reality itself, a concept strikingly similar to the Taoist idea that perception and awareness shape experience.

This chapter explores the fascinating connection between quantum mechanics and Taoism, showing how both systems of thought embrace uncertainty, fluidity, and the mysterious role of the observer.

The Observer Effect: Does Looking Change Reality?

One of the strangest discoveries in quantum physics is that the very act of observing something changes what is being observed.

The Double-Slit Experiment: A Taoist Paradox

The double-slit experiment is one of the most famous and baffling experiments in quantum mechanics. It reveals how particles, such as electrons or photons, behave differently when observed.

When unobserved, particles act like waves, spreading out and creating an interference pattern.

When observed, they behave like particles, following a specific path.

This means that the mere act of looking at a quantum system changes its nature. But why? How does simply observing something force it to behave differently? Scientists still do not fully understand this, but Taoism has long suggested that the world does not exist in a fixed state—rather, it is shaped by awareness and perception.

In Taoist philosophy, reality is not rigid; it is a flowing, ever-changing experience. Just as water takes the shape of its container, quantum particles seem to take the shape of our interaction with them.

The Uncertainty Principle: The Limits of Knowledge

Another strange discovery in quantum physics is the Heisenberg Uncertainty Principle, which states:

> *"You can never simultaneously know both the exact position and the exact momentum of a particle."*

This means that at the smallest scales of reality, there is an inherent uncertainty—not just because of technological limits, but because nature itself does not allow absolute precision.

Wu Wei and the Uncertainty of Reality

Taoism teaches that certainty is an illusion. Instead of trying to control or define reality, we must embrace its fluid nature. This is exactly what quantum physics is now proving—the deeper we look, the more uncertain things become. Laozi describes this perfectly:

> *"Those who know, do not speak. Those who speak, do not know."*

This aligns with Heisenberg's discovery that knowing one aspect of reality prevents us from knowing another. Just as Taoism teaches us to let go of the need for absolute knowledge, quantum mechanics reveals that ultimate certainty is impossible.

Taoism and Wave-Particle Duality

Quantum physics has also revealed that light and matter exist in two states at once—both as waves and as particles. This is known as wave-particle duality, and it is one of the fundamental mysteries of nature.

As a wave, light spreads out and moves through space like ripples in a pond. As a particle, light behaves as discrete packets of energy (photons).

This duality is a perfect parallel to the Taoist concept of Yin and Yang—two opposing forces that are not separate, but complementary. Light is not just a wave or a particle—it is both, depending on how we observe it.

Similarly, in Taoism:

Life is *both* chaos and order.

Existence is *both* form and emptiness.

A person can be *both* strong and soft.

Quantum physics has confirmed what Taoism has long understood: duality is not conflict—it is balance.

Does Consciousness Shape Reality?

Some scientists have taken the observer effect even further, suggesting that consciousness itself might play a role in shaping reality. This idea is controversial, but it aligns with the Taoist belief that awareness is an active force, not a passive one.

The Role of Mindfulness and Intention

Taoist practices such as meditation and Qi Gong emphasize the idea that focused attention can influence the world around us. Modern research into the placebo effect and the power of intention suggests that our thoughts do have a measurable impact on our health and experiences. Experiments in quantum physics have hinted at similar ideas:

Delayed Choice Experiment: This suggests that decisions made in the present can affect events in the past, implying that time itself may not be as fixed as we think.

Quantum Eraser Experiment: This shows that observation can retroactively change how particles behaved in the past.

While mainstream science is still debating the implications, these findings suggest that consciousness and reality may be more deeply connected than we realize.

Taoism has always embraced this mystery, recognizing that perception is not just a passive experience—it is part of how reality unfolds.

Embracing the Unknown: The Tao of Uncertainty

Both Taoism and quantum mechanics teach us that the nature of reality is deeply uncertain—and that's not something to fear. Instead, uncertainty is a fundamental part of how the universe works.

The Tao is undefined and cannot be fully grasped. Quantum particles exist in multiple states until observed. The more we seek certainty, the more it slips away. The Tao Te Ching encourages us to surrender to the unknown rather than resist it:

> *"The more you grasp, the less you hold.*
> *The more you control, the less you*
> *master."*

Similarly, quantum physics teaches us that trying to force absolute knowledge results in paradoxes. Instead of struggling against uncertainty, we should flow with it—just as Taoism teaches.

The Quantum Tao

Quantum physics and Taoism both reveal a universe that is fluid, interconnected, and shaped by observation.

The Observer Effect shows that reality changes based on how we look at it. The Uncertainty Principle proves that absolute knowledge is impossible. Wave-particle duality mirrors the Taoist principle of Yin and Yang. Consciousness itself may influence reality, aligning with Taoist teachings on awareness.

Taoism has long taught that reality is not something we can fully control or define—but something we can flow with. Modern science is now beginning to confirm this truth.

In the next chapter, we will explore the interconnected nature of the universe and how quantum entanglement reflects the Taoist idea that everything is one.

8 THE INTERCONNECTED UNIVERSE— TAO AND ENTANGLEMENT

Everything Is One: Vision of a Connected Reality

Taoism has always taught that everything in the universe is deeply connected. The Tao Te Ching describes existence as a web of interdependent relationships, where nothing exists in isolation. Modern science is now proving that this ancient idea was right all along.

In the field of quantum mechanics, one of the most baffling discoveries is quantum entanglement—a phenomenon where two or more particles become linked, no matter how far apart they are. When something happens to one particle, the other reacts instantly, even if they are light-years away.

Albert Einstein famously called this "spooky action at a distance" because it defies classical physics. However, for Taoism, this is not strange at all—it perfectly aligns with the belief that all things arise from the same source (the Tao) and remain connected.

This chapter explores how quantum entanglement, the unity of nature, and Taoist philosophy all point to a fundamental truth: separation is an illusion. Everything is part of a greater whole, moving in harmony with the Tao.

The Science of Quantum Entanglement

Quantum entanglement is one of the most counterintuitive discoveries in physics. When two particles become entangled:

Their states are linked, no matter how far apart they are. Measuring one instantly affects the other—faster than the speed of light. There is no known force transmitting this effect—it just happens.

This goes against everything we understand about how information and energy travel. According to Einstein's theory of relativity, nothing should be able to influence something else faster than the speed of light. Yet, entanglement happens instantaneously.

Taoism has long suggested that the universe does not operate through isolated parts, but through a continuous, interwoven fabric of existence. Entanglement provides scientific evidence that everything is connected at a fundamental level.

Taoism and the Illusion of Separateness

Laozi wrote:

> *"The Tao is great. Heaven follows the*
> *Tao. Earth follows Heaven. Man*
> *follows Earth."*

This passage describes a hierarchical yet unified flow of existence, where all things are connected by an unseen force. Quantum entanglement reveals that this is more than just poetic wisdom—it is a scientific reality.

In Taoist thought, the belief that we are separate individuals, distinct from nature and others, is an illusion. Instead, everything arises from the same source and remains connected even when physical distance separates us.

Web of Life: Nature's Evidence for Entanglement

The concept of interconnectivity isn't limited to quantum physics. It is also seen throughout nature.

Mycelial Networks: The Internet of Trees
Beneath the soil, fungal networks connect trees and plants, allowing them to communicate and share nutrients. A tree under attack by insects can send chemical warnings through the network, helping nearby trees defend themselves. This interwoven ecosystem mirrors quantum entanglement, where separate beings act as part of a greater whole.

Bird Flocks and Fish Schools: Instant Coordination
Birds in a flock and fish in a school move as one, reacting instantly to changes in direction. Scientists have found that their reactions are faster than what normal sensory communication allows, suggesting an invisible field of connection. This mirrors the way entangled particles communicate instantly, even across vast distances.

Human Consciousness and Collective Awareness
Studies in psychology and neuroscience suggest that human emotions and thoughts can influence others beyond direct communication. Phenomena like group intuition and shared emotions in large crowds indicate a deeper, unseen connectivity.

Taoism teaches that consciousness is not confined to the self—it flows through all things, just as the Tao does.

The Tao of Cosmic Intelligence
Does the Universe Think? Some scientists speculate that the entire universe behaves as an interconnected system of information. This idea is strikingly similar to the Taoist concept that the universe is a living, flowing intelligence.

Physicist John Wheeler suggested that reality might be a self-observing system, where everything affects everything else. Some interpretations of quantum mechanics propose that the universe processes information like a vast consciousness. This aligns with Taoism's idea that existence is not a collection of separate objects, but a flowing, self-aware whole.

Laozi wrote:

*"All things arise from Tao. They grow
and return to the source. Returning to
the source is peace."*

This suggests that existence is cyclical and interconnected, just as modern physics is beginning to understand.

Implications for Human Life: Living in Flow with Tao

If everything is interconnected, how should we live? Taoism offers three key lessons:

Let Go of Ego and Individualism

Since everything is connected, the idea of an isolated "self" is an illusion. Our well-being is tied to others, nature, and the greater whole. The more we embrace this, the more we live in harmony with the Tao.

Trust in the Natural Flow

Taoism teaches that life moves in patterns that we cannot always see. When we resist, we create struggle. When we trust, we move with ease. Like quantum particles, we are part of a vast, unseen network—we just have to let go and flow with it.

Cultivate Compassion and Mindfulness

If everything is connected, our actions affect more than just ourselves. Every thought, every action ripples out through the web of existence. Practicing kindness, mindfulness, and balance aligns us with the natural order of the universe. The

Universe Is One, and We Are Part of It

Both Taoism and modern physics suggest that we do not exist as separate beings, but as interconnected expressions of a greater whole.

Quantum entanglement proves that distance does not separate reality—everything remains linked. Nature itself mirrors this interconnectedness, from forests to animal behaviour to human consciousness. The Tao flows through all things, connecting them in unseen but undeniable ways. The more we understand this, the more we can let go of resistance, trust in the flow of life, and embrace our role in the cosmic web.

In the next chapter, we will explore how Taoism's ancient energy practices align with modern science, revealing how breathwork, meditation, and movement tap into the fundamental forces of the universe.

9 THE TAO OF LIFE—HEALTH, LONGEVITY, AND ENERGY PRACTICES

The Body, Mind, and the Flow of Nature

For centuries, Taoists observed that those who lived in harmony with nature seemed to enjoy longer, healthier lives. They developed practices—focused on breath, movement, stillness, and adaptability—to align the body and mind with the natural rhythms of existence.

Today, modern science is uncovering surprising parallels between these ancient practices and cutting-edge research in neurobiology, longevity science, and quantum biology. Taoist health practices were not based on superstition but on careful observation of how energy flows through living systems.

This chapter explores how Taoist principles of breathwork, movement, and meditation align with modern understandings of nervous system regulation, brain function, and long-term health.

Energy, Oxygen, and Longevity

Taoist breathwork, known as "nourishing the breath" (Sheng Qi), has been practiced for thousands of years to enhance vitality, regulate emotions, and extend lifespan. While these ideas may have once seemed mystical, scientific research now confirms that how we breathe profoundly affects our health.

Breath and the Nervous System
Deep, controlled breathing stimulates the vagus nerve, activating the parasympathetic nervous system (rest-and-digest mode) and reducing stress. Taoist breathing techniques mirror modern breathwork therapies like diaphragmatic breathing, which lowers cortisol levels and heart rate.

Oxygen, Carbon Dioxide, and Longevity Studies on hypoxia (low oxygen exposure) show that controlled breath-holding can trigger cellular repair mechanisms, much like certain Taoist breath techniques.

Balancing CO_2 and oxygen intake is now known to enhance cellular function and mitochondrial efficiency—key factors in longevity.

Taoist "Embryonic Breathing" and Modern Research
Some Taoist meditation masters practiced "Embryonic Breathing," a technique that minimized external breath movement while enhancing internal oxygen efficiency.

This is remarkably similar to modern hypoxic training, which athletes use to boost endurance and stimulate anti-aging pathways.

Movement and Longevity: Taoist Science of Flow
Taoist masters understood that movement was not just exercise—it was a way to cultivate energy and maintain health. They developed Tai Chi and Qi Gong, gentle movement practices that promote balance, flexibility, and resilience.

The Power of Continuous Motion
Unlike high-impact exercise, Tai Chi emphasizes circular, flowing movements that reduce joint strain while improving muscle coordination and circulation.

Studies show Tai Chi improves balance, lowers fall risk, and enhances brain function—especially in older adults.

The Science of Fascia and Energy Flow
Modern research reveals that fascia (the body's connective

tissue network) plays a key role in movement, flexibility, and even energy transmission. Taoist movement techniques engage and stretch fascia, improving blood flow, reducing inflammation, and maintaining mobility over a lifetime.

Micro-Movements and Longevity
Taoist philosophy teaches that small, consistent movement keeps the body vital. Studies on longevity hotspots (like Okinawa and Sardinia) show that the world's longest-living people engage in lifelong low-intensity movement, mirroring Taoist practices.

Stillness and the Brain: The Tao of Meditation
Taoism doesn't just emphasize physical movement—it also highlights the power of stillness. Taoist meditation techniques focus on quieting the mind, calming the body, and allowing natural energy to flow.

Meditation and the Brain
Neuroscience has confirmed that meditation enhances neuroplasticity, improves focus, and slows brain aging. Studies show that long-term meditators have more grey matter in key areas of the brain, reducing cognitive decline.

The Taoist Concept of "Emptiness"
Taoists describe meditation as entering a state of Wu (emptiness)—where mental chatter disappears, and awareness becomes clear. Modern research shows that deep meditation reduces activity in the Default Mode Network (DMN)—the part of the brain responsible for overthinking and stress.

The Power of Stillness in Stress Reduction
Chronic stress is linked to inflammation, aging, and disease. Taoist inner stillness practices reduce stress hormones and promote a state of physiological repair and balance.

Practical Applications: Living in Harmony with Tao
Taoism teaches that longevity and health are not about forcing

the body to do more—but about flowing with nature's rhythms.

Breathwork for Daily Energy
Practice deep, slow breathing to regulate stress and increase oxygen efficiency. Use breath retention techniques (like those in Tai Chi) to enhance cellular repair.

Movement as a Lifelong Practice
Engage in gentle, flowing movement (Tai Chi, Qi Gong, or slow walking) to maintain energy flow and flexibility. Avoid rigid, high-impact exercise that causes excessive strain.

Embracing Stillness and Rest
Incorporate meditation or quiet time to allow the body and mind to reset. Follow natural rhythms—wake with the sun, sleep early, and rest when needed.

The Taoist Approach to Health and Longevity
Taoism offers a timeless approach to well-being that aligns perfectly with modern scientific discoveries.

Breath, movement, and stillness regulate energy flow and extend healthspan. The body is a self-balancing system—when we follow its rhythms, we thrive. By harmonizing with natural cycles, we can cultivate vitality, clarity, and resilience.

In the next chapter, we'll expand beyond the human body and explore the cycles of the cosmos—how Taoist philosophy aligns with astrophysics and the ever-changing universe.

10 THE CYCLES OF THE COSMOS—TAO AND ASTROPHYSICS

The Universe in Constant Motion

Taoism has always embraced the idea that everything in the universe is constantly changing, shifting, and cycling. From the microcosm of a single atom to the vast expanse of the universe, Taoists have long understood that the cosmic order is not static but rather a flowing, dynamic process.

In Taoist thought, everything has a cycle: birth, death, and rebirth—with each phase linked to the others in an ongoing dance of energy, transformation, and balance. This reflects the interconnectedness of all things, and Taoist philosophy teaches that we must live in harmony with these natural cycles to achieve balance and well-being.

Modern astrophysics is beginning to echo these ancient truths, revealing that the universe itself is governed by cycles of expansion and contraction. The Taoist idea of the eternal return—that all things are constantly reborn in new forms—parallels our understanding of cosmic cycles that span billions of years.

This chapter explores how Taoist ideas of cyclical change relate to current astrophysical discoveries, from the Big Bang to the Big Crunch and the potential future of our universe.

Taoist Cycles and the Big Bang

The Taoist idea of cycles is reflected in the Big Bang theory, which suggests that the universe began in a massive explosion from a singular point of energy, known as a singularity. From this event, the universe expanded and continues to do so, stretching out its galaxies, stars, and planets across vast distances.

The Tao of Creation: The Eternal Cycle

Taoism teaches that creation comes from the "void"—the undifferentiated state of existence, known as Wu Ji, which is akin to the singularity that preceded the Big Bang. The moment of creation is seen as a shift from emptiness to form, much like how Taoism speaks of the Tao manifesting into the material world.

Energy, Balance, and the Expanding Universe

As the universe expands, it mirrors Taoist concepts of Yin-Yang—one force stretching outward while the other contracts inward, both maintaining balance.

The expansion of the universe could be viewed as Taoist creation, an ongoing unfolding of the Tao—the spontaneous, natural force that permeates and drives all things.

The Big Crunch: The Return to the Void

While the universe is expanding, scientific theories suggest that one day it may begin to contract in what is known as the Big Crunch. This scenario imagines a future in which the universe collapses back on itself, ultimately returning to the singularity from which it was born.

Taoism and the Return to Emptiness

Taoism teaches that all things return to the source—the emptiness from which they came. In Taoist thought, this cycle of creation and destruction is not a tragedy, but a natural, harmonious process.

The Big Crunch could be understood as the universe returning to Wu Ji, the unmanifested state, only to begin the cycle of creation anew.

Cosmic Rebirth

Just as Taoism celebrates the constant rebirth of life, the collapse of the universe could lead to another cycle of creation, an eternal cosmic flow where nothing is lost—everything transforms into a new form, just as the Taoist idea of Wu Wei (effortless action) emphasizes the transformation of energy without waste.

The Cycles of Life, Death, and Rebirth

Taoist philosophy not only applies these grand cosmic cycles to the universe but also to the cycles of life and death. Taoism sees life as an ongoing flow—birth, growth, death, and rebirth—where each phase is interconnected and necessary for the next.

The Cosmic Cycle of Rebirth

Taoism sees the universe as a reflection of the human experience, where death is not an end, but part of the natural cycle of transformation.

Modern physics acknowledges that energy is neither created nor destroyed, only transformed, mirroring Taoist teachings about the impermanence of all things and the constant flow of energy through different forms.

The Tao of Death

Taoism teaches that death is not to be feared but accepted as a natural cycle—the energy that once formed a living being simply transforms into something else, continuing the flow of the Tao.

In the universe, stars undergo life cycles where they are born, shine, and eventually collapse into black holes, only to transform again, perpetuating the endless cosmic cycle.

The Ever-Changing Nature of the Universe

The Taoist view of the universe emphasizes the constant change of all things. This aligns closely with the second law of thermodynamics, which states that systems move toward greater entropy, or disorder. However, this disorder isn't random—it is part of a greater flow, constantly moving toward new states of being.

Entropy and the Flow of Energy

Just as the universe expands, it also grows more complex, with energy flowing in new directions and creating new forms. Taoism sees this as the ebb and flow of energy, where the universe naturally moves from one state to the next, always in balance.

This entropic process can be understood as a natural unfolding of the Tao, a constant cycle of energy transformation and balance.

The Tao of Cosmic Harmony

While the universe is always in motion, Taoism teaches that there is an underlying harmony in the cosmic flow, despite appearances of chaos. Every cycle, every transition, and every phase of the universe is part of the greater Tao.

Universal Interconnectedness

Taoism teaches that everything is interconnected, whether it's the planets and stars or the energy in a human body. This view aligns with the principle of cosmic harmony found in astrophysics, where the universe functions as a unified whole, with each part influencing the others.

Taoism, Harmony, and the Future of the Universe

Whether the universe continues expanding, contracts, or oscillates between these states, the Tao will remain, maintaining the balance of all things. Like the Taoist principle of Wu Wei, the universe's movements occur effortlessly, without forced direction, yet always moving toward harmony.

Living in Tune with the Cosmos

The Taoist teachings about cycles and cosmic harmony are not just about the universe—they offer a profound way of understanding our place in the cosmos. Just as the universe follows patterns of expansion, contraction, and transformation, we too must live in harmony with these natural rhythms to find peace and fulfillment.

As we've seen in this chapter, modern science increasingly supports the Taoist worldview, where energy, balance, and cycles govern everything—from the tiniest particles to the largest cosmic structures. By understanding and aligning ourselves with these natural cycles, we can cultivate a deeper sense of connection with the universe and enhance our well-being.

In the next chapter, we'll explore how this interconnectedness extends beyond the material world and dives deep into the nature of consciousness and the Tao.

11 LIVING IN HARMONY—APPLYING THE SCIENCE OF TAO

Bridging Ancient Wisdom and Modern Life

As we've explored throughout this book, Taoism offers profound insights into the natural flow of the universe, emphasizing the importance of energy, balance, and interconnectedness. These principles have deep roots in the fabric of both the material world and the unseen forces that shape reality—forces like energy, vibrations, and cycles. But how does this knowledge apply to our everyday lives?

Can we truly live in harmony with the Tao—in a way that aligns us with both the natural world and the evolving demands of the modern age?

In this chapter, we'll explore how the science of Tao can guide us toward a more harmonious existence, not just by understanding the universe, but by applying these principles to our thoughts, our actions, and our relationships.

The Flow of Life: Effortless Action (Wu Wei)

One of the central teachings of Taoism is the concept of Wu Wei, which is often translated as "effortless action." It's the idea of living in a state of natural flow, where actions align with the spontaneous flow of life and the forces around us, rather than forcing things to happen.

Modern psychology and neuroscience have found that flow states—the moments when we feel fully immersed in an activity, with time seeming to disappear—are aligned with peak performance. When in a flow state, we are at our most creative, productive, and adaptable. This state of effortless action is deeply connected to Taoist philosophy.

Wu Wei teaches that when we act in harmony with the natural flow, we don't waste energy on friction or resistance. Instead, we work with the forces around us, much like how water naturally flows around rocks in a stream.

By understanding the science of flow, we can better embrace Wu Wei in our own lives, moving effortlessly with the rhythm of the world around us.

Body Balance: Bioelectricity and the Tao of Health

Taoism teaches that the body is a microcosm of the universe, and just as the cosmos operates in a balanced, harmonious flow, so too must our bodies. The ancient Taoists understood the importance of balance—specifically the balance of Qi (life energy), and this balance is as much a physical reality as a philosophical one.

Bioelectricity, the electric charges that flow through our body's cells and tissues, is a vital force that powers our thoughts, actions, and functions. Science now shows that these bioelectrical signals play a key role in regulating everything from our muscle contractions to the transmission of nerve impulses.

Taoist practices like acupuncture and Tai Chi are designed to promote the free flow of energy through the body, restoring balance when it's disrupted. These practices stimulate the bioelectric fields, helping to realign the body's energy flow and promote health and healing.

Incorporating Taoist practices into modern health regimens—whether through meditation, breathing exercises, or physical movement—can help us stay in tune with the natural rhythms of our bodies and foster long-term well-being.

Interconnectedness and Empathy

The Tao of Relationships: Interconnectedness and Empathy
One of the most important aspects of Taoism is the idea that everything is interconnected—not just in the physical world, but also in the realm of human relationships. Every action, every word, every gesture creates a ripple effect that flows through the fabric of society, affecting not only those around us but also our environment and even ourselves.

Just as quantum mechanics shows that particles can be entangled—linked together in such a way that a change in one will affect the other, regardless of distance—human beings are also deeply interconnected. Our actions influence each other, our thoughts affect the world around us, and our emotions are shared by those in our sphere of influence.

Taoism teaches that compassion, empathy, and balance are essential to living harmoniously with others. By aligning ourselves with the principles of interconnectedness, we can cultivate better relationships and contribute to the greater good.

Just as the entangled particles in quantum theory communicate across vast distances, our actions and intentions create subtle effects in the world. Taoism encourages us to be mindful of these effects and to act with intention and compassion in our daily lives.

Living with the Rhythms of Nature

Taoism emphasizes the importance of living in harmony with nature, understanding the subtle rhythms of the natural world, and respecting the cycles of life, death, and rebirth. In our fast-paced, modern world, it's easy to become disconnected from these rhythms. But reconnecting with nature can lead to a more peaceful, balanced existence.

Research in biophysics and neurobiology has shown that humans are deeply influenced by the rhythms of nature—from the daily cycles of light and dark (circadian rhythms) to the seasonal changes that affect our mood and energy levels.

Taoism teaches that by aligning our lives with nature, we can tap into the natural flow of energy that exists all around us. By living in tune with the seasons, the cycles of the moon, and the natural environment, we can create a life that is more balanced and harmonious.

The Science of Tao: A Path Forward

As we've seen in this book, the ancient wisdom of Taoism and the latest findings in quantum physics, bioelectricity, and cosmology are not opposites—they are deeply interconnected. Both reveal a universe of energy, cycles, and balance, where the flow of life, matter, and consciousness operates in a harmonious and interdependent system.

In our personal lives, this knowledge offers us a practical roadmap for creating a life of balance, harmony, and effortless flow. By applying Taoist principles to our actions, relationships, health, and environment, we can create a more fulfilling and harmonious existence—one that is in tune with the natural world and the universal rhythms that govern all things.

Living the Tao

The ultimate goal is not just intellectual understanding but practical application. By embracing Wu Wei, seeking balance, cultivating compassion, and reconnecting with the cycles of nature, we can live the Tao in our daily lives. The science of Tao isn't just about understanding the universe; it's about living in alignment with it.

By living consciously and intentionally, we become part of the greater flow, contributing to the harmony of the world around us and living in peace with the Tao.

12 THE WAY FORWARD: LIVING THE TAO

Throughout this book, we've uncovered striking parallels between Taoist teachings and scientific principles—from the flow of Qi to the laws of physics that govern the universe. By observing the deep connections between energy, vibrations, cycles, and interconnectedness, we begin to see that the universe is a vast, dynamic system in which balance and harmony are not just ideals but actual forces at work.

The principles of Taoism, such as Wu Wei, Yin-Yang, and the Tao of Qi, offer more than just philosophical musings; they provide us with tools for living in a way that aligns us with the natural flow of the universe. In a world that often feels fragmented and chaotic, Taoism provides a timeless guide to living in balance with the forces of nature, the rhythms of life, and the interconnectedness of all things.

Science, in its search for the fundamental truths of the universe, is beginning to confirm what Taoism has long suggested: that energy, vibrations, and balance are the forces that shape not just the physical universe but also our minds, our bodies, and our lives.

By applying Taoist principles—whether through understanding the flow of energy, embracing effortless action, or recognizing the interconnectedness of all things—we can begin to live more consciously, more harmoniously, and more aligned with the universal rhythms that govern all existence.

In essence, the science of Tao is not about discovering something new; it's about rediscovering what has always been true. The Tao is not just a teaching of the past—it is the living principle that underlies everything, and it is waiting for us to embrace its flow.

In a world increasingly driven by technology and information, we may sometimes forget that the most profound discoveries come not from external sources, but from our ability to tune into the world around us and listen to the subtle whispers of the Tao. By living with intention, mindfulness, and respect for the universal laws that govern all things, we can find peace, clarity, and connection in a world that is often overwhelming. As you step forward on your journey, remember that the Tao is not a destination—it is a path. It is a flow that invites us to live in harmony with the universe, to trust in the effortless action of life, and to understand that, like the universe itself, we too are part of the greater Tao.

Live in the *flow*.

Live in *balance*.

And remember, the Tao is always with *you*.

REFERENCES

Taoist Texts and Philosophy:
- Laozi. *Tao Te Ching: A New Translation*. Translated by Stephen Mitchell, HarperOne, 1988.
- Zhuangzi. *The Book of Chuang Tzu*. Translated by Martin Palmer, Penguin Classics, 2006.
- Chang, David K., ed. Tao Te Ching: A New Translation. Tuttle Publishing, 2004.
- Watts, Alan. *The Way of Zen*. Pantheon Books, 1957.

Scientific Foundations and Quantum Theory:
- Bohm, David. *Wholeness and the Implicate Order*. Routledge, 1980.
- Capra, Fritjof. *The Tao of Physics: An Exploration of the Parallels Between Modern Physics and Eastern Mysticism*. Shambhala, 1975.
- Capra, Fritjof. *The Web of Life: A New Scientific Understanding of Living Systems*. Anchor Books, 1996.
- Greene, Brian. *The Hidden Reality: Parallel Universes and the Deep Laws of the Cosmos*. Knopf, 2011.
- Maxwell, James Clerk. *A Treatise on Electricity and Magnetism*. Clarendon Press, 1873.
- Bohr, Niels. *Atomic Physics and the Description of Nature*. Cambridge University Press, 1934.
- Planck, Max. *The Universe in the Light of Modern Physics*. Dover Publications, 1958.

Energy, Vibration, and Flow:
- Byrne, Rhonda. *The Secret*. Atria Books, 2006.
- Braden, Gregg. *The Divine Matrix: Bridging Time, Space, Miracles, and Belief*. Hay House, 2007.
- Lipton, Bruce. *The Biology of Belief: Unleashing the Power of Consciousness, Matter, and Miracles*. Hay House, 2005.

Energy Practices and Taoist Methods:
- Huang, Chungliang Al. *The Tao of Tea: Wisdom from the Ancient World*. Tuttle Publishing, 1997.
- Roth, Harold D. *Original Tao: Inward Training (Nei-yeh) and the Foundations of Taoist Mysticism*. Columbia University Press, 1999.

Astrophysics and Cosmic Cycles:
- Sagan, Carl. *Cosmos*. Random House, 1980.
- Hawking, Stephen. *A Brief History of Time*. Bantam Books, 1988.
- Tyson, Neil deGrasse. *Astrophysics for People in a Hurry*. W.W. Norton & Company, 2017.

ABOUT THE AUTHOR

Clayton Tonkin is a passionate artist and thinker, deeply influenced by the teachings of Taoism. His journey with Taoism began after reading a book that profoundly shifted his perspective on life, especially during a challenging time in his life. This shift in thinking sparked his interest in exploring how ancient wisdom can be applied to modern-day challenges, helping others find balance, clarity, and flow in their lives.

Through his books, Clayton seeks to share the timeless wisdom of Taoism in a way that resonates with people today—offering guidance, insight, and practical ways to live in harmony with the natural rhythms of life. His work is rooted in the belief that by embracing simplicity, letting go of control, and aligning with the flow of life, we can experience profound transformation.

Clayton is committed to bringing the wisdom of the Tao to a wider audience, believing that these teachings have the power to bring peace, creativity, and deeper understanding to anyone willing to listen.

THE CREATIVE TAO: FLOW, EXPRESSION, AND EFFORTLESS INSPIRATION

Just as the universe flows effortlessly through cycles of creation and transformation, so too does human creativity. In the next book, *The Creative Tao: Flow, Expression, and Effortless Inspiration*, we will explore how the same principles of energy, balance, and spontaneity that shape the cosmos also guide the artistic process.

Where The Science of Tao examines the forces that govern existence, The Creative Tao shifts the focus inward—into the realm of imagination, intuition, and artistic expression. By understanding how Wu Wei (effortless action), Qi (life energy), and Yin-Yang balance influence the creative process, we can break free from struggle and learn to create with ease, authenticity, and flow.

Creativity is not about control—it is about allowing. Join us on the next journey, where ancient wisdom and modern insight come together to reveal the art of effortless creation.

FINAL THOUGHTS

The journey through Taoism and science is not about reaching a definitive answer—it is about learning to see the world with fresh eyes. The Tao is not a puzzle to be solved but a rhythm to be experienced, a flow that connects all things, from the smallest quantum particle to the vastness of the cosmos.

Understanding the Tao does not require force, nor does it demand belief. It simply invites you to observe, to reflect, and to move with the natural currents of existence. Science seeks patterns; Taoism recognizes harmony. Where one measures, the other flows. Where one seeks to explain, the other invites you to experience. Yet, at their core, both point to the same truth: everything is interconnected.

As you move forward, consider how you might embody this wisdom—not as something external to grasp but as something already present within you. In every breath, every thought, every interaction, the Tao unfolds.

Your path will continue, and with it, new questions will arise. But in the space between those questions, in the silence between moments, the answer has always been there.

Let go. Flow. Trust.

The Tao moves with you.